MILK TRANSPORT

NIGEL SCAIFE

AMBERLEY

Front Cover: One of two Burg-Hobur tankers used by Arla Foods for cream collection, a 6,000-gallon tank with three compartments each holding 2,000 gallons, MX05 EHT is seen parked on the scales at Arla Foods, Stourton, West Yorkshire.

Rear Cover: Volvo FL J39 LCP was based at Settle, North Yorkshire, and was driven by the author for Cravendale Foods, which was the manufacturing side of Associated Dairies, carrying mainly cream in a three-compartment tank to reduce frothing: 1,000 gallons at the front, 500 gallons in the middle and 2,000 gallons at the rear. During its life at Settle it wore two other liveries: MD Foods and Arla Foods. It was purchased by South Caernarfon Creameries, who used it on farm collections.

First published 2019

Amberley Publishing
The Hill, Stroud
Gloucestershire, GL5 4EP

www.amberley-books.com

Copyright © Nigel Scaife, 2019

The right of Nigel Scaife to be identified as the Author of this work has been asserted in accordance with the Copyright, Designs and Patents Act 1988.

ISBN 978 1 4456 8826 8 (print)
ISBN 978 1 4456 8827 5 (ebook)

British Library Cataloguing in Publication Data.
A catalogue record for this book is available from the British Library.

Origination by Amberley Publishing.
Printed in the UK.

Introduction

To begin with, many farms kept cows inside towns and cities and milk was distributed around houses by a cowkeeper using a horse and cart.

In 1864, an outbreak of rinderpest in London led to a shortage of milk supplies in the city. George Barham, the son of a London dairyman, formed the Express County Milk Supply Company. Barham had the idea of sourcing his milk from farms in rural areas and transporting it into the city.

At first milk was carried on passenger trains in churns, but as demand grew, separate milk trains were introduced from the 1890s. By 1885 Express was bringing 30,000 gallons of milk into the capital every night.

Barham's enterprise was such a success that other firms established milk collection depots at railway stations, and then sent all the milk to the towns and cities by rail. By the 1900s the Great Western Railway was carrying 25 million gallons of milk a year from the West Country to London. The last regular milk train to run in Britain was in 1980.

Throughout the country, churn stands became standard at the end of every farm lane, awaiting collection by the churn lorry; these were four-wheel flatbed lorries which most often became double-decked to carry those extra few churns.

The Milk Marketing Board (MMB) was set up in 1933 to control the distribution of milk by buying the milk from the farmers at a fair price and then selling it on to the dairies across the nation. In 1994 the MMB was disbanded and Milk Marque came into existence; however, Milk Marque was then divided into three co-operatives in 2000.

The first experiments in farm tanker collection took place with the Scottish MMB in 1954, in the Kirkcudbright area. The experiment was a great success and the following year the MMB started a pilot scheme in Berkshire. Two bulk tankers were thought to do the work of five churn lorries.

Doorstep deliveries in the early years were first carried out with a hand cart; however, demand grew and required a larger and quicker mode of transport, so horses and carts were used up until the early 1960s. Electric milk floats were then introduced for those early morning deliveries, as they were quiet, suiting operations in residential areas. In 1967 there were 55,000 battery-operated vehicles in total on the roads.

Today's milk is collected from the refrigerated farm vat by farm collection tankers, then either delivered straight to the dairy, or reloaded into larger tankers which hold up to 29,000 litres for distance deliveries.

How It All Started

My interest in milk transport all began when I started driving a tanker for Associated Dairies in March 1991. I'd always been interested in taking photos of lorries prior to this time, but working in the surroundings of other milk tankers got me taking more and more of them. Soon after the end of the Milk Marketing Board in 1994 there was a flood of Milk Marque tankers into the industry, which meant a whole new different-liveried tanker to photograph. Milk Marque brought out a fleet list booklet with all the names that were on the side of the tankers, which I took an interest in, visiting various depots around the country and taking the opportunity to capture more photographs. The likes of Gordon Blunden, PM Photography, Peter Davies and Richard Baker were selling photos and it became so interesting to see other milk-related vehicles, old and new, entering my growing albums. All my other friends that are into lorry photography started to realise my interest in milk transport, and started photographing them, then sending the photographs over to me; each and every one of them has been fantastic at coming up with new material for me. Over the twenty-eight years I've been involved in milk transport so far there have been many changes, with hauliers losing contracts and gaining contracts, that it's been hard work keeping up to speed with everything nationwide. And not only the transport side of things – the dairies have also changed dramatically over the years; so many lost, acquired and changed names. This is something I've also tried to keep an interest in, recording dairy history and how times have changed. I've met so many good friends throughout this interest of mine, which you could say is worldwide, and I must thank you all for the help and support each and every one of you has given me, and I hope to meet many more in the future.

If anyone has any information they have which they would like to share, please contact me on nigelscaifemilktransport@gmail.com where I would be most grateful to hear from you.

Until the invention of the refrigerator, cows were kept in cities to provide fresh milk. Cowkeepers had the first means of transport for delivering their milk from their small farms in the cities and towns. The milk from each milking would be put into a large churn then ladled out into small cans as they went down each street, door to door. Curtis Bros was established in 1799 and was formed in Surrey, with operations later in Balham, Ewell, Epsom and Effingham.

A handcart owned by Welford's Dairy, which had branches in all districts of London. The company was established in 1845 by Richard Welford, a cowkeeper from Holloway, north London, who took over Warwick Farm near Paddington. Welford's had the largest retail milk business in London and supplied Queen Victoria. In 1915 Welford's joined United Dairies which, from 1959, became part of Unigate.

A well-loaded United Dairies horse-drawn cart would have been seen on many of the streets of London. This one is seen at Drayton Gardens in the 1940s. Normally the driver would sit on the front box and use the foot rest. (Supplied by Bob Malcolm)

Express Dairy had a very large presence in London, the milkman in the uniform giving a good company image. The four-wheeled C type cart is lettered to No. 1 Thornton Avenue, Chiswick, with fleet No. 279. George Barham was the company founder, in 1864, when it was called the Express County Milk Supply Company.

An Albion A10 chain-driven 3-ton lorry from around 1914 picking up milk churns for United Dairies Wholesale Ltd.

An articulated Albion of United Dairies Wholesale, Banbury, fully loaded with 10-gallon churns, had a maximum speed of 12 mph. The chain-driven tractor was permanently attached to a Carrimore trailer.

This Curtis & Dumbrill articulator was photographed after takeover by United Dairies Wholesale, sometime after 1926 – the same year C&D opened a new bottling plant at Valley Road, Streatham, south London. The tractor and trailer were manufactured by Scammell.

Plenty of helpers to unload the churns from the Albion of Ayrshire-based Cumnock Creamery Company. The churns would be labelled with the farmer's name and the number of gallons delivered would be recorded for payment. Each churn would also be 'sniffed' to check for the quality of the milk.

Bottle distribution from Valley Road, Streatham, to all the smaller distribution depots in and around London would have been undertaken by these Scammells. This one was fleet number UD 1036, seen in 1928. (Supplied by Bob Malcolm)

Scammell chain-driven motive unit YR 6996, with fleet number UD 902, looking brand new in December 1926. The side door is for easier access for unloading the crates of milk. The trailer reads 'Pasteurised Fresh Milk', with 'Sold Under Licence With The Authority Of The Minister For Health' below. (Supplied by Bob Malcolm)

In the 1920s the Great Western Railway (GWR) used Thornycrofts to collect milk churns and bring them to centralised collection points. These were called transfer stations, used for loading the churns onto rail vans to take to dairies in the cities. During this period, 17-gallon conical churns were used and when full each would have weighed 2.5 hundredweight.

A Great Western Railway Thornycroft loading 10-gallon milk churns into a 'Siphon' railway van, where they would be double stacked. The open-slatted sides would keep the milk cool during transportation. The body on the Thornycroft was demountable for other types of work.

C. T. Clark, Transport Contractor of Wrexham, loading up with 17-gallon steel churns on a Thornycroft to be taken to the nearest railway station for delivery to the dairies in the city.

United Dairies chain-driven Scammell, fleet number 955, with a glass-lined tank, which was more hygienic for cleaning out when empty. This is a frameless design built by Scammell, who pioneered this type of tank – one of the manufacturer's most important contributions to lorry design. Capacity in this one was 2,100 gallons, equal to about 12 tons.

Road-rail tanks were used from 1931 to the 1960s. Sixty were designed and built by R. A. Dyson of Liverpool and carried 2,000 gallons. They would be cleaned and loaded, then transported to the railway yard. At the train's destination, they usually had a short journey by road to the dairy. The first rail journey operated was from Bruton to London. This tank was probably empty as it's being pulled by an empty lorry. Note the solid tyres.

Another Dyson road-rail tanker loaded on to a purpose-built rail wagon. This was done by winching the tank trailer on by the ballast tractor, then guiding it into a position where it could be locked into place and chained down. Note the pneumatic tyres. An unrestored six-wheel road-rail tanker is extant at the Didcot Railway Centre, built in 1947 by the Great Western Railway.

At Express Dairy, Morden, milk arrived at the dairy in these 1937 LMS-built 3,000-gallon tanks. The number W44198 indicates it was allocated to the Western Region of British Railways. It's being shunted by an Express Dairy 0-4-0 built by Hunslet of Leeds.

British Railways built this six-wheeled 3,000-gallon milk tanker in 1952 for Express Dairy. Express and Unigate were the last to use these railway tankers. It was photographed at the North Yorkshire Moors Railway in 2009.

United Dairies 1959 Scammell Highwayman TMR 513 with a 3,000-gallon tanker passing Hammersmith Underground station, west London. This lorry was based at Wood Lane, London. (PM Photography)

DMW 812, a 1946 Scammell of United Dairies, was also based at Wood Lane, London. This and other Scammells were double-shifted out to Wiltshire to collect 3,000-gallon loads. (Peter J. Davies)

United Dairies 1951 Scammell WMY 344, coupled to a bottle-carrying van, is heading down the bottom of the M10. This 24-tonner worked out of Scrubs Lane and Wood Lane dairies. (Peter J. Davies)

A newly painted Unigate Scammell unloading full crates at Lea Valley Dairies, Burr Street, Luton. WWT 313 worked from 1952 up until 1974 and was based at Scrubs Lane, close to Wood Lane Dairy, London. After 1974 it worked on internal shunting duties until 1982. (Peter J. Davies)

Miers Transport of Bradmoor, Wolverhampton, ran this Karrier Victor churn lorry. JW 976 was owned and driven by Reg Miers, who joined forces with Midland Counties Dairy in 1966. Midland Counties Dairy started in 1913 with an experimental dairy owned by the White family. (Supplied by the late Dennis Miers)

James Kirby began trading as a cowkeeper from Chatham Street in Leicester city centre. This Kirby & West Bedford WHL, dating back to 1933, is loaded with 17-gallon steel churns as well as 10-gallon steel churns on the purpose-built roof carrier. (Richard Baker)

A Horlicks Dairies 1962 Commer, 275 PYC, with a full load of new churns. These lorries would have collected two loads of churns in the morning, then delivered crated bottled milk in the afternoon out to their Rooksbridge dairy, Somerset. Horlicks Dairies bought out Cheddar Valley Dairy in 1958, which had been in business since the 1880s.

J. H. Willis was founded in 1926. This Albion KL 127 petrol-engined lorry seen working in the 1930s is pictured with a mix of empty churns heading back from Liverpool to Wrexham. (Richard Willis)

CYB 966J, a 12-ton Bedford, loaded up with empty churns for the next day's collection. This was captured at Unigate, Wootton Bassett. The dairy first opened in 1908 as the Dairy Supply Company and merged with United Dairies in 1915. (Adrian Cypher)

Registered LMV 252 in 1945, this Scammell is seen loaded with 10-gallon churns. It later passed into preservation and has retained its United Dairies livery. (Richard Tew)

W. Macfarlane & Son from Kirby Lonsdale, south Cumbria, would have visited many farms in the area with this five-cylinder 1948 ERF, fitted with a Jennings V type cab, delivering churns to the local dairies of Barbon, Settle and Libby's at Milnthorpe and Kendal.

A North of Scotland Milk Marketing Board Albion Chieftain, AS 2669, pictured in 1956 with a double deck for churns. When these 10-gallon churns were full, they would weigh 130 lb (59 kg) each. Note the women loaders.

This Commer, AG 6624, belonging to hauliers Houston Bros, was registered in 1931. This picture shows the empty churns stacked up to the front after delivering to the city of Glasgow. The return load would consist of food and other goods for the company's home town of Cumnock.

Healds Dairy was started by brothers Robert and James Heald in 1893. In 1900 the dairy moved to Ford Bank Farms, Didsbury. This Dennis Condor, UND 438, shows the trademark of the 'leaping happy cow' on the front of the cab. Healds of Didsbury was bought out by Waterford Foods of Hyde who, in 1998, merged with Avonmore Foods to form Glanbia.

T. H. Goodwin & Sons of Whitchurch came up with this novel idea for the changeover period from churns to bulk collection: a 1,000-gallon tank at the rear and a platform at the front which would carry fifty-four churns. Albion WNT 422 was registered in 1961.

YYA 422, a 1957 Bedford D6LO diesel, is pictured loading up pint bottles in metal crates at Oakdale Creameries in November 1958. Oakdale Creameries became South Coast Dairies, which was taken over by United Dairies, which later became Unigate. (Supplied by Bob Malcolm)

Miers of Bradmore, Wolverhampton, was the third haulier to start farm collection by tanker in England, on 1 September 1957, at Mr T. G. Cambridge's farm, Blymhill, Staffordshire. The 1957 Albion, UJW 500, was a 1,750-gallon, two-compartment tanker. (Supplied by late Dennis Miers)

On the arrival of a Co-Operative Wholesale Society (CWS) tanker at the dairy, the quality control staff would have plunged the milk before taking the sample to achieve the correct butterfat sample. You can see the plunger protruding from the manhole on 1946 Thornycroft, HXY 459.

This 1950 AEC, MPB 756, of the Milk Marketing Board (MMB), is seen at Llangefni Creamery, Anglesey. The MMB was formed in 1933 to control milk production and distribution in the United Kingdom.

The CWS chose this AEC Mercury to be its first bulk farm collection tanker to go into operation.

This CWS 1953 AEC Mammoth Major Mk III is having its load sampled, whereby it is dipped with the dipstick to check the quantity being delivered. These dipsticks were unique as they were calibrated to their own tanks.

AEC Mammoth Major eight-wheeler flat CXE 837 was new to Pickfords in 1936. It was shortened, as seen here, and fitted with a tank, being out-based at Chippenham and doing daily bulk runs into London with haulier H. Tideswell of Kingsley, Stoke-on-Trent, which had been operating since 1924.

This Express Dairy AEC Mammoth Major Mk V, 197 ALE of 1960, was photographed at the Lorry Driver of the Year Contest, which was hosted by Express at their Victoria Road, South Ruislip, depot. The ladder used to climb to the top of the tank doesn't look easy. (Peter J. Davies)

Parked on the fuel pumps at South Ruislip depot is 1963 AEC Mammoth Major Mk V 103 FXF. This model became a big player in the Express Dairy fleet. The fleet number, 2937, gives an indication of just how many vehicles the company ran. (Peter J. Davies)

The Co-Op fleet was made up of a large number of ERFs. TNB 683K worked out of Cricklade depot, near Swindon. Today, this vehicle is in preservation as a wrecker. (Adrian Cypher)

London Co-Operative Society (LCS) 1963 Scammell Highwayman 542 BAN is seen on the North Circular, London, no doubt heading back to its dairy at Palmers Green. (PM Photography)

This Milk Marketing Board 1963 Albion, 3824 PJ, is coupled to a 2,500-gallon tank mounted on a Scammell Fourtrack semi-trailer. The cab's nameboard had slots for a board indicating the destination of the load; in this case it was Express Dairy, Cricklewood.

One of a pair of AEC Mammoth Major Mk Vs, 386 YPK of 1962 is seen parked at the transport depot of the Milk Marketing Board, Newbury. This was the depot where the MMB's very first farm collection tanker ran from, known as the Newbury Pilot Scheme, on 1 February 1955.

AEC Mandator FPL 531J, looking very new, loading up at the Milk Marketing Board depot at Bamber Bridge, Lancashire, which was founded in 1936. The two-compartment tank would have a gross weight of 32 tons.

Two new Albion Clydesdale farm collection tankers, APK 540H and APK 541H, on the tanker reception point at MMB Bamber Bridge. In 1969/70 milk churn lorries were unloading their churns in the other half of the milk reception. Bamber Bridge had a very large fleet of tankers in operation at this time.

Milk Marketing Board Albion Clydesdale BPF 152H was operated from Keighley depot, which served Settle Creamery, West Marton Creamery and Leeds Dairy. This shot was taken in the town of Skipton. (PM Photography)

PPK 348E, a Leyland of the Milk Marketing Board, being loaded with plastic-crated pint bottles for distribution around north-west Lancashire from Bamber Bridge Dairy. The Boalloy-built body on 40-foot York tandem running gear would be able to carry 936 crates of milk bottles. The Tautliner curtains are pulled right around the front of the trailer to assist easier loading.

John MacFarlane of Kirkby Lonsdale, Cumbria, used two retired road tankers for transporting milk and skim. A 2,500-gallon tank from a Dodge and an 1,800-gallon tank from an Albion Chieftain were bolted to a 36-foot flat, hauled by Guy Big J 4T CEC 917S. (The late Eddie Heeley)

This Ford D series Chinese Six, HER 876N, from Bridge Farm Dairies, Mildenhall, Suffolk, would have carried crated bottled milk on the very strangely styled body.

Lancashire Dairies Ford Transcontinental DNF 223T, taking a break on the services. It would be delivering the Super Life flavoured milk produced at the dairy, which, years ago, was called Lancashire Hygienic Dairies. The company closed the dairy, which was at the back of Strangeways Prison, in 2002.

This AEC Mercury, OHJ 568P, of Lord Rayleigh's Farms would have picked milk up from its own farms, which date back to the Strutt family in 1873. In 1960 it was the first dairy in the country to change over completely from glass bottles to Tetra Pak cartons at their Hatfield Peverel Dairy in Essex. (Raymond Jenkins)

Longley Farm was founded in 1948 by brothers Joseph and Edgar Dickinson and is still in operation at Holmfirth, West Yorkshire. AEC Mammoth Major BAK 499L is now in preservation in this original livery. (The late Jim Taylor)

S. J. Bargh of Caton, near Lancaster, was established by Samuel James Bargh, who started transporting milk in churns from farms to local dairies in 1935 from his home near Lancaster. The business then grew from this and is still running today in the very distinctive green livery. This is Scania 111 ORN 70P. (The late Eddie Heeley)

N. H. Garden of Rossett, Wrexham, was a pig farmer. Norman would carry whey from Reece's Creamery at Malpas to supply his own pigs. ERF UON 623S with a Gardner 180 engine was captured at Dickinson's, Holmfirth. (The late Jim Taylor)

Haulier G. A. Stamper of Culgaith, Penrith, with a 6 x 2 Seddon Atkinson 401, XRM 850Y. The tank had a load of milk from Langley Farm, Holmfirth. G. A. Stamper started tanking milk from the 1960s until they closed down. Their dispersal sale was held on 3 November 2001. (The late Jim Taylor)

This Aberdeen Milk Marketing Board Leyland Freighter, H554 USA, had a Primrose second axle fitted to allow 14,000 litres to be carried in the tank, built by W. P. Butterfield of Shipley. The Aberdeen Milk Marketing Board dairy was called Twin Spires and at the time ran fifteen tankers but closed in 1994. (Alec Syme)

This pair of John Maitland Leyland Freighter Chinese Sixes, E25 UUS and D126 OCS, were both new to McKechnie Motors of Girvan in a green livery. Maitland started churn collection in 1930 and was one of the first private hauliers in the area to begin bulk tanker collection, in 1960. (Bill Reid)

This Leyland DAF 60 in Robert Wiseman livery is pictured on the intake bay at Bellshill in 2001. The Chinese Six was new to Aberdeen Milk Marketing Board and was able to carry 14,000 litres.

Mitchells of Inverurie was established in 1928 and had passed through four generations when the business was transferred over to Graham's Dairy in 2014. The Leyland Freighter 1718 used to be owned by Aberdeen Milk Marketing Board. G576 PSO was purchased to move the milk from the farm to the dairy, which was only a mile away. This Chinese Six is now in preservation.

Leyland Clydesdale VUS 680W of James McKinnon Jr of Kilmarnock was a typical Scottish tanker which used hydraulic operated pumps as opposed to the English vacuum tanks, hence why the Scots used to have a more squared tank. McKinnon started out in milk transportation in 1931 and this lasted until they lost the Scottish Milk contract in 1999. (Alec Syme)

Tennant of Forth started the collection of milk in cans from the late 1920s. They had a separate depot at Sandilands, Lanarkshire, where twelve bulk tankers were based. This tank, on the back of Volvo FL6 G358 NNS, had been on two other chassis; the first was Albion Clydesdale BVD 243J. (John Tennant)

DAF 1900 G937 SST, from the Claymore Dairy at Nairn, which was originally owned by the North of Scotland Milk Marketing Board in the early 1930s. In December 1998, 51 per cent of the business was sold to Express Dairies and it is now owned by Graham's Dairy, Bridge of Allan.

Claymore Creamery on the Orkney Islands ran a pair of Volvo FL7s in 1997. N233 CBS is pictured here; the other was N162 CBS. Since the creamery opened in 1946 it has produced milk for the islands, plus cheese and ice cream recently.

Thomas Paisley Niven was founded in 1926 and started with a 1-ton Ford petrol-powered lorry. In 1927 the firm won a contract with Dalbeattie District Farmers to collect milk from farms and deliver it to Dalbeattie Creamery. This Volvo FL6, F323 TBK, started out as a flat and later had a Thompson tank fitted which would carry 9,700 litres.

Shetland Farm Dairies was formed in 1994 when the dairy farmers of Shetland bought the creamery from the previous owner, Kennerty Dairy. This is L862 MSO, their 7.5-ton IVECO, which, in 1997, did three trips around the islands collecting milk.

Bridge of Allan is the home of Graham's Dairy, a family-run operation founded in 1939 by Robert Graham. Mercedes 2524 M318 SNN was captured in June 2001.

McKechnie Motors (Girvan) sold their lorries, including this Leyland Freighter, to Maitlands of Trabboch after the Scottish Milk Marketing Board rationalised milk collection. Carntyne took over the rest of the McKechnie Motors business in 1994. (Alec Syme)

Bibby Distribution ran this Leyland DAF 18-tonner from their Kendal depot. P565 YGB was working on the Scottish Milk contract, collecting milk from the South Lakes and south Cumbria.

P. & M. E. Coates of Ulpha, south Cumbria, used this Volvo FL6 in Butler Farmhouse Cheese livery, which is from Inglewhite, Lancashire. D63 KND was new to North Western Carriers, Mobberley, Cheshire, then was handed to Payne's of Ripon before ownership by Coates. With these previous two owners it had pulled a drawbar trailer.

J. M. Ridley ran this MAN from its Allendale depot, Northumberland. When it closed down, Davidsons of Coundon took over the milk collection. (The late Richard Scott)

A Payne's Farm Dairies Scania 92 waiting to unload cream at MD Foods, Settle. Charles Payne first moved to Ripon in 1972 with his father; they farmed 100 cows there and started bottling milk for their delivery round.

The transport side of the Milk Marketing Board became Dairy Crest, which then became Dairy Products Transport. This Leyland Clydesdale in the distinctive MMB blue livery was photographed unloading at Northern Foods, Wakefield. (The late Jim Taylor)

This Leyland Clydesdale two-compartment tanker, based at Keighley depot, West Yorkshire, was one of the first to be changed into the white Dairy Products Transport livery. (The late Jim Taylor)

After the Leyland Clydesdale, the Leyland Freighter became the predominantly operated farm collection tanker for Dairy Crest Transport. A855 GPE was based at Wakefield and was captured on the CIP (Clean In Place) bay at Northern Foods, Wakefield. (The late Jim Taylor)

Dairy Products Transport started to try short trailers for the tighter spots where a six-wheeled rigid would struggle; these were nicknamed mini artics. The tank behind DAF 2300, J262 VAW, would carry 15,000 litres.

An ERF E14 of Dairy Products Transport is parked at Dickinson's, Holmfirth. E319 JPF was running at 38 tonnes, which gave a 24,000-litre payload. Dairy Products Transport once had forty-five depots throughout England and Wales. (The late Jim Taylor)

This Ford Cargo drawbar outfit, working at 32 tonnes, is refuelling at Keighley depot. D565 XPE was one of several Ford Cargos that Dairy Products Transport ran. (The late Jim Taylor)

Transhipment of three four-wheelers into two artics on Barden Moor, west of Catterick. All these tankers were from Northallerton depot. Once the artics were loaded, they frequently took their loads up to Associated Dairies or the Co-Op, both with dairies at Newcastle-upon-Tyne. (PM Photography)

C801 FHK was the first Ford Cargo built and trialled for Dairy Crest and was successful, as over the next three years more appeared on the fleet. At 32 tonnes gross, the Ford would carry 8,500 litres and the drawbar trailer 11,500 litres, which meant two trips to the parked trailer. (PM Photography)

Volvo FL7s unloading at the Co-Op at Llangadog, in Carmarthenshire. The dairy opened in 1957/8 and was latterly run by Associated Co-Operative Creameries, part of the CWS, then in 2004 by Dairy Farmers of Britain, but closed in late 2005.

This Associated Co-Operative Creameries DAF 2100 was on the wash at Merrybent depot, which was a transport-only depot west of Darlington. F430 FUJ would have started out with Dairy Products Transport, then Milk Marque before ACC.

H288 BEA was owned by W. Freeman, Curdworth, Warwickshire. The ERF ES6 was on a contract for collecting milk around Leicestershire and Warwickshire for the Midlands Co-Op dairy in Birmingham. Freeman's started milk collection back in the 1930s.

Long Clawson was founded in 1911, when twelve Vale of Belvoir farmers formed a co-operative to produce Stilton cheese in the village of Long Clawson. This DAF 2300, H253 AWV, was bought new by C. T. Newton of Nottingham. The Crossland-built tank would carry 14,500 litres.

H878 OUX of J. H. Willis from Gresford, Wrexham, was purchased second-hand from Ryder, Droitwich. The 14,500-litre Massey-built tanker was photographed when it was working from Llangefni, Isle of Anglesey.

This Dansco-liveried Volvo FL7, E721 FPK, was operated by Mansel Davies but was new to Dairy Products Transport. Dansco's dairy was based at Newcastle Emlyn, Carmarthenshire, where they have been making cheese since 1900.

A load being collected from Whittingham Hall Farm, Goosnargh, Lancashire, by Volvo FL10 N237 YNC from Lancashire Dairies. The milk would then be delivered to their only dairy, in the centre of Manchester.

D. W. Weaver of Park Farm, Endon, Stoke-on-Trent, started in 1964 with the acquisition of four vehicles employed on milk churn collection for MMB. This DAF 85CF was collecting milk on behalf of Joseph Heler Cheese.

Wincanton's XYC 516X, named *River Fowey*, is in the 'Flying W' livery and is coupled to a tri-axle trailer tank from the 1960s. Most of these were converted to tandem axles by the 1970s. Wincanton first invested in two tankers in 1933 for milk haulage and in 1942 acquired a national milk contract with the MMB. (PM Photography)

Wincanton's Leyland DAF 75 was parked at Wootton Bassett depot, which once had eighty-five tankers; by 2000 there were ten. M527 ALG is seen lifting milk for Unigate.

P132 BFC, a DAF 75 in Wincanton livery collecting for Unigate, was photographed on the pumps at Unigate Creamery, Totnes. The creamery was originally owned by Dawes Dairy in 1934. (Pat Crang)

Wincanton Foden Alpha T27 UBD, with rear-steer, was one of a batch of nine with numbers from T21 to T29 which was operated at Aldermeads, Wincanton, and the Unigate dairy at Totnes. (Pat Crang)

William Armstrong of Longtown, Cumbria, ran this second-hand Scania 93, F891 OJF, which mainly worked with a drawbar trailer collecting milk for Nestlé at Dalston. Armstrong was established in 1927 but started milk haulage in 1928 with a Model T Ford.

D. W. Weaver's X971 ULG, a Foden Alpha 3000 with a 16,000-litre Massey tank, was one of the first to be mounted on a tumbler bar at the rear. It is seen in 2004.

N373 YBU, in Express livery, was run by Arla Foods from their Appleby transport depot, which closed in 2009. Appleby dairy had operated in various guises since 1931, when farmers sent their milk to Newcastle, then later to London. It also supplied milk to the Express cheese plant at Appleby, which had been open since 1959.

T492 KAU was based at Express Dairies, Ashby-de-la-Zouch, Leicestershire, and liveried to the Milk Group, which was formed in 1994 after the deregulation of the MMB. Ashby dairy was part of the merger with Arla Foods in October 2003. The dairy closed in 2014.

During 2001 Lloyd Fraser had made significant gains with Milk Marque, acquiring their Telford, Wrexham, Four Crosses, Wakefield and Droitwich collection contracts. The client split into three companies, Axis, Zenith and Milklink, which saw Fraser take on further contracts with Axis and Zenith in Dalton (Thirsk) and Anglesey. This sleeper cab DAF 2700, H556 FNR, was based at Gaerwen depot, Anglesey.

Tankfreight operated this ERF ES8 at Clitheroe depot, Lancashire, on Zenith milk collection. R660 GUA was a very short wheelbase tanker which grossed at 21 tonnes with a 12,000-litre carrying capacity. Zenith Milk started trading in April 2000, one of three co-operatives created from the Government's forced break-up of Milk Marque.

Dalton depot ran drawbar outfit P585 EHN, which was operated by Tankfreight, lifting milk for Zenith. The IVECO EuroTech was on the weighbridge at Arla Foods, Kirkstall Road dairy, Leeds. The lorry's tank was named *Hutton Ambo* and the trailer *South Mimms*, both after castles.

Tankfreight owned three of these combinations when new, which were later transferred over to Lloyd Fraser, operating at Gaerwen depot. They were registered N324 EUM and N326 EUM, seen here when owned by Fraser on for Zenith Milk, plus N325 EUM. These 40-ton outfits would carry 8,500 litres on the lorry and 16,000 litres on the trailer.

M154 FNH, a Volvo FS7 and short tank operated by United Transport, collecting milk for Axis from their Thame depot. All United tanks were named after National Trust sites, this one being named *Greenlands*. These were referred to as mini artics.

Gregory Distribution won a contract with Milk Marque in 1994. This Mercedes 1831 drawbar outfit, N491 RTT, was captured at North Tawton, Devon. Milk Marque started with just three depots, at Torrington, Crediton and Chard. All Gregory's tanks were named after tors; these were *Combe Tor* and *Great Tor*, and the trailer was *Colard Tor*.

Gregory's Mercedes M713 MFJ was in the Taw Valley Creamery livery when seen at North Tawton depot, Devon; the creamery, which was opened in April 1974, is almost next door.

Milklink-liveried Scania WJ02 KCG. This drawbar combination was new in this shot and is still in use up to the present day. It is operated by Gregory Distribution at North Tawton. The haulage firm was started in 1919 by Archibald John Gregory.

Just in from its morning round at Longslow Dairy Group's depot at Llandudno Junction, North Wales, is this twenty-seven-year-old electric Morrison float.

Express Dairies G901 MHE is seen at Express's Long Lane dairy, Aintree, Liverpool. It was part of a large batch of G-registered Yorkshire Electric Vehicles (YEV) which operated in the Merseyside area. The dairy was originally owned by Hanson's Dairies.

West Midlands Co-Operative Society, Walsall, opened its dairy on Midland Road on 10 July 1937. It ran a large batch of these Smiths S95D 2-ton models. KDH 246D was fleet number 785 and was withdrawn from service on 1 July 1966. (Claire Pendrous)

Kirby & West from Leicester built its own milk floats, YJF 63 being one of them from 1960. In 2007 Kirby & West ceased the production of its own milk but still continues delivering milk to doorsteps throughout Leicestershire.

Planks of Poulshot, Devizes, ran KBB 855X. This Smiths float is currently having an overhaul before going back into its electric fleet, delivering milk between 30 and 55 miles daily.

Ipswich & Norwich Co-Op float BPV 667T is a Smiths 'Cabac' with a thirty-six-cell battery and original cab. The Ipswich & Norwich Co-Op was sold to Dairy Crest in 2008. Smiths was founded in 1920 in Newcastle-upon-Tyne where, in the 1950s and 1960s, they focused on manufacturing milk floats. (Paul Luke)

This Wales & Edwards Rangemaster of Unigate was captured in Littlehampton on its daily round. The Wales & Edwards factory was at Harlescott, Shrewsbury, and built three models of milk float, which did speeds of 14, 17 or 20 mph with a distance range of between 30 and 40 miles.

N. J. & C. C. Bristol of Clitheroe, Lancashire, doing the rounds in a Smiths electric float. NBV 606X came new to Clitheroe. The area was being covered by two private rounds men and this float did 22 miles a day. The Smiths float took eight hours to fully charge, which gave it a range of 25 miles.

Pattemores Transport of Misterton, Crewkerne, Somerset, was established in 1938. It was an early operator of the original Steyr-cabbed ERFs, including N574 AYB, seen transferring its load into its trailer before picking up its own load. (Pat Crang)

A Cummins-powered ERF ES8 of G. Easton & Son with a 12,000-litre trailer. L879 NEG was the last drawbar outfit which Easton operated. The company was founded in 1938, starting out by taking churns directly to the Co-Op dairy with a Ford Model T. (Ian Moxon)

South Caernarfon Creameries, Chwilog, Gwynedd, ran DU09 EPE, a Crossland-built tanker that could carry 14,000 litres on the DAF CF and 12,500 litres on the trailer. SCC started milk production in 1938, and cheese production in 1959.

Peninsula Milk of Oakhampton was using C. C. James Tankers for its milk collection with this Mercedes 2534 drawbar outfit, N964 YNV. Peninsula Milk was acquired by Milklink in 2003. It was sold to Robert Wiseman in 2006, who finally closed the dairy in 2011.

C. T. Newton Ltd of Nottingham ran this very different combination of a single-axle drawbar behind Leyland DAF 2300 H253 AWV. The combination grossed at 31 tonnes with the trailer able to carry 5,200 litres. (Dave Stretton)

V55 MOT, *Earl 'O' Stair*, a Volvo FM7 with pump belonging to John Maitland from Trabboch at their yard at Mauchline, Ayrshire. In 1989 the Scottish Milk Marketing Board wanted to rationalise milk collection for south-west Strathclyde from three hauliers to one. Maitland won the contract over McKechnie of Girvan and Thomas Mulroy of Prestwick.

At the end of the MMB in 1994, S. J. Bargh signed a contract with MD Foods to collect their milk. M55 SJB was one of two drawbar outfits which made two daily trips to MD Foods at Bamber Bridge near Preston.

Longslow was established in 1947 and processed milk in Market Drayton, and latterly at Colwyn Bay. PN02 JFO was one of three drawbar outfits; each could carry 27,000 litres and operated between farms at Wrexham and Stafford until the company closed in October 2005.

T. J. Slater of Longridge, Lancashire, started out with a Volvo F12 moving whey, and later on other milk products, until 2007. X188 RFR was photographed in the snow at the 'hole in the wall' at Beattock on the M74.

An unusual combination belonging to G. A. Stamper of Culgaith, Penrith. This ERF E14, G666 MRM, with an ex-farm 9,000-litre collection tank, was used for small loads of sweetened condensed milk from Nestlé at Dalston, Cumbria. (Pat Crang)

Ernest Kidd of Lancaster had just moved from its Melling depot in 1978. URN 683R is a Gardner 240-powered ERF coupled to a 'banana tank' which normally needed extra flexi-hose to reach the outlet pipe half way up the tank. (The late Eddie Heeley)

Daisy Dairy was the result of a merger between North East Lancashire Co-Operative Dairies in Oswaldtwistle and United Co-Operative Dairy in Hyde, Cheshire. E144 NBV was just dropping down into Dickinson's at Holmfirth. (The late Jim Taylor)

This Milk Marque-liveried ERF, H226 PUJ, operated by Ryder from Kendal, is seen taking transhipment from two Ryder farm collection tankers. This photo was taken in the Bull Beck layby at Caton, near Lancaster. (PM Photography)

J. E. & A. Taylor of Penwortham, Preston, Lancashire, ran this gas-powered ERF ECX. The gas tanks were so tall that a sleeper pod was built to help disguise them, hence the name on the front, *The Cruise Missile*. MK02 DFO was parked on the infamous 'stones' at the Bodfari Dairy, Chester, which is now owned by Meadow Foods.

Wensleydale creamery at Hawes in the Yorkshire Dales. This Scania P33 SJB was the tanker collecting milk from local farms. It held 14,300 litres and was operated by S. J. Bargh of Caton in Wensleydale livery. Cheese has been made at Hawes Creamery since 1897.

This double-drive Foden, DG53 AYV, was the first eight-wheeler to be added to the farm collection fleet of D. W. Weaver. The 20,000-litre tank was built by Massey and was operated from their Ashbourne depot on behalf of Dairy Farmers of Britain. (Ian Moxon)

Express Dairies Leyland DAF 45, a 7.5-tonner, would have been delivering glass bottled milk and other products around the franchised rounds men and independent bottle milk suppliers for the household doorstep. V877 EJA was photographed at Stoke-on-Trent depot, 15 May 2004.

Unigate had a division called Chill Chain, which was for distribution of products to convenience stores, forecourts, hospitals, schools and caterers. V637 NWC was captured loading up at their Portsmouth distribution depot.

This Leyland DAF 90, J134 XUJ, of Central Dairies, part of the Longslow Food Group, was based at Newton depot and is seen doing store deliveries in Aberystwyth.

A Sottish Milk Marketing Board Leyland Marathon, YGG 318S, with its trailer liveried to Galloway Creamery, Stranraer, where cheese has been made since 1850. The creamery is now owned by the French company Lactalis, who purchased it from McLelland in 2005. (Alec Syme)

Unigate Dairies lightweight Ford unit G843 CJH had an unladen weight of 4,070 kg. It is seen coupled to a refrigerated bottle trailer at Totnes dairy in Devon. (Pat Crang)

Unigate's D253 ONM, an ERF E10 with a sliding door refrigerated bottle trailer, parked on Fleet services. This will be heading home to their London dairy. (Pat Crang)

This Northern Dairies Renault, coupled to a trailer without a refrigerator, was mainly used on pasteurised and sterilised milk bottle deliveries. B852 EKY would have been based at Hull. (The late Jim Taylor)

A Dodge Commando, B591 SUM, of J. & E. Dickinson, Holmfirth. Longley Farm is the name of the original holding near Holmfirth, where the dairy is still based. (The late Jim Taylor)

An Arla Foods Scania, T288 JBV, at the Bamber Bridge site with a 'Douglas the Butterman'-liveried fridge on supermarket deliveries. Arla Foods closed the Bamber Bridge dairy in April 2004 after sixty-eight years of production.

Scania NJ12 WCO, pulling a Gray & Adams-built combination trailer which acts as a fridge and a tanker. The top deck part of the body can accommodate eighty-five cages or twenty-two pallets for outward-bound loads. The tank, at lower level, can hold 19,000 litres and was built by Crossland. This combi trailer would receive a transhipment from an eight-wheeled bulk farm collection tanker.

A Renault G340, M761 JDF, with a chassis-mounted fridge for chilling the Cotteswold Dairy's products. Harry Workman founded Cotteswold Dairy in 1938, when it was just a 30-gallon milk round. Their dairy in Tewkesbury is run by the third generation of the family.

A well turned out Renault Magnum, CD10 PAD, with its Gray & Adams double-deck fridge plugged in ready for the nightly trunk to Gearwen on Anglesey, which was operated six nights a week.

Rodda's Clotted Cream MAN WK58 AZD in the old livery, which was changed in 2014. Eliza Jane Rodda started making clotted cream from the family's farmhouse kitchen in Scorrier near Redruth in 1890 and it's been a family affair ever since.

Bates Dairy has been manufacturing since 1939 and is Merseyside's largest independent dairy. CN54 BRX is one of an all-DAF fridge fleet, plus twenty electric floats.

Express Dairies W526 JOG was one of a large batch of Volvos, which was its preferred lorry at the time. This FM was on supermarket deliveries from the Wythenshawe dairy, which Arla Foods acquired in 2003 and closed in 2009, after operating for sixty-two years.

Claymore Dairies at Nairn ran G788 UAS, a sixteen-year-old DAF 1900 with a demountable fridge. Claymore has had several owners, being originally owned in the early 1930s by the North of Scotland Milk Marketing Board, which had distribution depots in Dingwall, Fort William and Wick.

Dairy Crest at Aspatria, Cumbria, ran four of these drawbar outfits collecting milk for the cheese plant. T284 MND, a rear-steer 320 CF DAF, could carry 15,400 litres and 10,000 litres in the trailer.

A Wm. Armstrong Scania P360 in the livery of Meadow Foods, just after transhipping its load into an artic. PX10 BXC was in a batch of four tankers built by Crossland, the others being BXD, BXE and BXF. Meadow Foods started in 1992 as a farmer-backed dairy trading business, which three years later merged with Bodfari to enter dairy processing.

A Buckleys Dairy DAF CF from Denby Dale, Huddersfield. The company started in 1989 and is still producing milk in glass bottles for West Yorkshire and beyond. YD62 SJV was captured in Derbyshire, where three eight-wheelers are lifting the milk for Buckleys.

Bartonsham Farm was started 150 years ago in 1869 at Hereford by the Matthews family with one cow and one wheelbarrow. They use Scania P340 WA06 BLF, which used to be owned by Gregory, for collecting milk.

OMSCO is the Organic Milk Supply Co-Operative, which was set up in 1994 by a small group of farmers to market their own organic milk. It now has over 200 farm members across the whole of the UK. WA08 DXE is contracted to OMSCO and operated by Gregory from their Sparkford depot, Somerset.

Parkham Farms started making cheese at Woolsery, Devon, in 1988. This Mercedes Axor, WU59 OUV, is one of three tankers in the fleet which picks milk up locally.

This Arla Foods ERF ECT was captured in the village of Bainbridge, near Hawes in the Yorkshire Dales. MX05 EEB was driven by the author on bulk loads of cream and skim, pulling a two-compartment tanker for the Arla Foods dairy at Settle, North Yorkshire.

Turners (Soham) had the contract for picking up milk for United Milk at Westbury, which opened for production on 1 June 2002. The ERF EC11, X597 UMA, was seen unloading ex-farm milk at Wyke Farms, Bruton, Somerset, where the original cheese recipe was created in 1861 by Ivy Clothier as a hobby. She used her husband's first cattle herd to produce the cheese.

Dairy Crest operated two of these farm collection tankers, each pulling three-axle drawbar trailers, from their cheese plant at Davidstow, Cornwall, which is the largest cheese plant in the UK. The tanks on KU57 JYD were built by Sayers, with a shortened trailer to keep inside the maximum legal length. This combination works out at 18,500 litres on the Volvo FM and 6,700 litres on the trailer.

Gregory Distribution bought a batch of twenty MAN TGA units and six were liveried with cow's names. WX07 AWR was named *Florence*; the others were *Marge, Bonnie, Daisy, Buttercup* and *Poppy*.

William Baines Transport of Ingleton, North Yorkshire, started milk transport with an 1,800-gallon tank on a Bedford TK, taking milk from Kendal to Huddersfield. Progressing through the years, Baines had contracts with various companies including Tankfeight and Milk Marque, working out of Penrith. A19 DWH was one of an all-Scania fleet.

Charlie Lauder Transport of Dumfries was pulling reload tanks on a regular basis for T. P. Niven of Palnakie. N17 CLT had just unloaded at Arla Foods, Settle, when it was photographed at the top of Buckhaw Brow on the A65, north of the town.

T. P. Niven Transport & Storage of Palnakie ran four of these DAF CFs. PX57 PXW was captured on its very first day of working for First Milk. It had just transhipped into a waiting reload trailer at Longtown, Cumbria, on 1 October 2007.

This Bibby Distribution DAF, PX09 ORW, was collecting milk for First Milk at Aspatria depot, Cumbria. It was liveried to First Milk's The Lake District Cheese Co., 'A Taste of the Lakes Since 1888'.

Jackson's Dairies of Hazel Grove, Stockport, runs a pair of DAF CF eight-wheel farm collection tankers. TA03 NKA was originally a 2009 plate belonging to Bibbys. Jackson's Dairies was established in the 1950s by Margaret and Alfred Jackson and currently delivers 500,000 bottles of milk a month, as well as lightweight clear containers, across the North West.

In 2012 Lloyd Fraser Group had been in business for twenty-five years but has only been hauling milk for eighteen of those years. PX12 RUR, with a Crossland-built tank, was captured at the depot at Dalton, North Yorkshire, which it had acquired in 2001.

Bibby Distribution has the First Milk contract. PX09 ORU is sitting in the sun at its depot at Castle Kennedy near Stranraer. The DAF CF is in the distinctive livery of Scottish Pride Family Cheddar. First Milk has four cheese dairies at Haverfordwest, Pembrokeshire; Aspatria, Cumbria; Campbeltown, Argyll; and Torrylinn on the Isle of Arran.

Sheep Milk UK from Laund Farm, Chipping, Preston, Lancashire, is a co-operative of farms who sell their milk, which then goes into making cheese. The firm's SF55 PGX is a former Wiseman tanker, which was captured heading back home to Chipping.

Wm. Armstrong of Longtown, Cumbria, used to be a main Hino dealer and put this 700 series, PX06 DTN, on the road to collect milk. It could carry 22,500 litres on behalf of Meadow Foods, who have processing plants at Chester, Holme-on-Spalding Moor and Peterborough. The Hino was converted to a 6x2 unit.

Mansel Davies of Llanfyrnach, Pembrokeshire, ran Volvo FL12 420 on various milk products from dairy to dairy. P9 MDS had just arrived back at Llanfyrnach depot to refuel. Mansel Davies is the largest milk haulier in Wales, collecting 1.5 million litres from over 450 farms each day.

WX56 BBK, *Galloway Marshall*, belonging to T. P. Niven of Palnakie, Dumfries and Galloway, was photographed after tipping its load of First Milk at Arla Foods, Settle. With the deregulation of the Scottish Milk Marketing Board in 1994, Niven successfully tendered for various contracts which developed into a new farm collection depot at Lockerbie.

Niven has opted for this concept vehicle, which has the pump and collection hose built onto the Scania unit for farm collection. This system can be used with slightly adapted reload tanks, which can be filled and dropped for a waiting tractor unit to forward it on to a dairy. SM16 OBC, *Galloway Flyer*, was captured at Dalbeattie depot.

John Mackirdy of Rothesay, Isle of Bute. This MAN, SB62 SZE, is on the CIP at Arla Foods, Settle. Mackirdy collects milk from the nine remaining farms on the Isle of Bute, which are all contracted to First Milk, all with one collection tanker which transfers the milk into a reload tank for mainland deliveries. Back in 1996 Mackirdy used to collect milk from thirty-six farms on the island.

Paul Coates is the owner of SF56 FLE, which is on contract to The Fresh Milk Company, which is responsible for milk procurement for The Caledonian Cheese Company at Stranraer. The lift axle on the unit and first axle on the trailer, along with the rear-steer, make this versatile outfit quite useful for farm collections in the Galloway region.

G. Stewart Jnr of Strathaven, South Lanarkshire, with Leyland Clydesdale WNS 533S queuing to tip at Scottish Farmers, Helen Street, Glasgow. Later, Stewart ran farm collection tankers in Robert Wiseman livery on contract.

Leyland Freighter 1618 of Scottish Road Service at Lockerbie, parked out on the road waiting to fuel up at the end of the day. G248 ESW was a very short wheelbase tanker, handy for farms with restricted access. (John Kerwin)

Scania MX59 EAA of Wensleydale Cheese at Hawes, returning home after passing the Ribblehead Viaduct on the Settle & Carlisle Railway. In 1992 Dairy Crest closed the creamery. However, six months later a team of four ex-managers, together with a local businessman, completed a management buyout.

A Stralis liveried to Dairy Farmers of Britain at one of their depots. The company, whose HQ was in Nantwich, was formed as a raw milk trading business (milk broker) in 2002 with the merger of the Milk Group and Zenith Milk, which went on to purchase Tyneside-based Associated Co-Operative Creameries. In 2009 Dairy Farmers of Britain went into receivership.

S. J. Bargh collecting milk on behalf of Wensleydale Creamery. PX64 TXN was captured at Thornton Rust, between Hawes and Aysgarth, in the Yorkshire Dales, with its Crossland-built 18,700-litre tank. Bargh was the first to use an eight-wheeled farm collection tanker in July 1999 with a Scania, T55 SJB.

Dales Dairies Scania BD61 DLF, which picks up milk locally for their dairy at Grassington in the heart of the Yorkshire Dales. William Oversby started the business in 1938, retailing to the local community, and it is now run by the third generation of the family.

Joseph Heler Cheese from Hatherton, Nantwich, Cheshire, has been producing cheese since 1957 from over 100 farms in a 45-mile radius. Scania P360 MV12 SNX is one of eight tankers that supply the dairy.

Unloading at Belton Cheese, Whitchurch, Shropshire, is part of the all-DAF fleet owned by Leigh of Loggerheads, which operates seven tankers for the newly named business to Belton Farm. The Beckett family has been making cheese with milk sourced from within a 25-mile radius of Belton Farm since 1922. T9, T999, K99 and T698 were all suffixed BBF.

A Dairy Crest Foden rear-steer which was based at Davidstow, Cornwall, sitting in the evening sun after transhipping its load into the trailer at Carland Cross in 2001. W208 JNA would carry 15,000 litres and the trailer 10,500 litres. Davidstow, at the time, was running a large batch of these, all consecutively registered.

The tanker the author first started driving back in March 1991 was this 1982 Leyland Freighter 1615 for Associated Fresh Foods at Settle, North Yorkshire. DUB 781Y was a four-compartment tanker which carried cream, with two 400-gallon compartments at the front and two 500-gallon compartments at the rear. This was to minimise the frothing during transport. Regular runs were made to Associated Fresh Foods at Accrington, Leeds, Newcastle-upon-Tyne and the West Marton Creamery near Skipton, North Yorkshire.

J787 VUX in Dairy Crest livery advertising Frijj, which is the flavoured milk drink produced at Sevenside, where this ERF E12TX 325 was based. The tank was a 32-tonner which had a piece added in the middle to be able to run at 38 tonnes. These tanks were nicknamed 'Long Toms'.

G. Easton of Alford captured at J. & E. Dickinson, Holmfirth, after tipping its load of milk from Lincolnshire. C163 XAH is a Leyland Cruiser with a 9,500-litre tank. The trailer was built by Lodge trailers of Liverpool. It was basically a chassis with re-used extended tanks. Its capacity was 12,000 litres. The trailer was built with a long A frame, which gave it good manoeuvrability. In fact, on a 90-degree turn the trailer would only cut in 9 inches. Six of these were operated. (The late Jim Taylor)

Acknowledgements

The majority of the photographs used in this book were taken by myself over a period of nearly thirty years, or are from my collection.

I would also like to thank all the hauliers and dairy companies that have allowed me to photograph the lorries which are used in this book.

I'd like to give a special mention to the following people, who have helped me with this book: PM Photography, Peter Davies, Raymond and Denise Jenkins, the late Jim Taylor, Pat Crang, Bob Malcolm, Alec Syme, Ian Moxon, Adrian Cypher, the late Eddie Heeley, the late Dennis Meirs, Claire Pendrous, Bill Reid, Dave Stretton, John Tennant, Richard Baker, Richard Willis, John Kerwin, Richard Tew, Paul Luke, and the late Richard Scott.